Pinball to Gaming Systems
Then to Now Tech

By Jennifer Colby

21st Century **Junior** Library
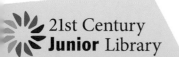

Published in the United States of America by
Cherry Lake Publishing
Ann Arbor, Michigan
www.cherrylakepublishing.com

Content Adviser: Adam Fulton Johnson, PhD History of Science and Technology, University of Michigan
Reading Adviser: Marla Conn, MS, Ed., Literacy specialist, Read-Ability, Inc.

Photo Credits: ©Gilmanhin/Shutterstock.com, Cover, 1 [left]; ©Anton27/Shutterstock.com, Cover, 2 [right];
©Everett Collection/Shutterstock.com, 4; ©Gilmanshin/Shutterstock.com, 6, 8; ©Atmosphere1/Shutterstock.com, 10;
©padu_foto /Shutterstock.com, 12; ©Matthew Corley/Shutterstock.com, 14; ©BlurryMe/Shutterstock.com, 16;
©Wachiwit/Shutterstock.com, 18; ©Gorodenkoff/Shutterstock.com, 20

Library of Congress Cataloging-in-Publication Data
Names: Colby, Jennifer, 1971- author.
Title: Pinball to gaming systems / Jennifer Colby.
Description: Ann Arbor : Cherry Lake Publishing, [2019] | Series: Then to now tech |
    Includes bibliographical references and index.
Identifiers: LCCN 2019004226| ISBN 9781534147263 (hardcover) | ISBN
    9781534148697 (pdf) | ISBN 9781534150126 (pbk.) | ISBN 9781534151550
    (hosted ebook)
Subjects: LCSH: Pinball. | Electronic games—History—Juvenile literature.
Classification: LCC GV1311.P5 C635 2019 | DDC 794.7/5—dc23
LC record available at https://lccn.loc.gov/2019004226

Cherry Lake Publishing would like to acknowledge the work of the Partnership for 21st Century Skills.
Please visit *www.p21.org* for more information.

Printed in the United States of America
Corporate Graphics

CONTENTS

Tabletop games like pinball were popular ways to pass the time.

A Tabletop Game

Have you ever played pinball? Tabletop games similar to pinball have been played since the late 1700s. But the modern pinball machine was **patented** in 1871 by British **inventor** Montague Redgrave.

The goal of pinball is to score as many points as possible.

Fun in a Box

Pinball is a coin-operated game. You put a coin in a slot and pull a plunger that shoots the ball into the game board. Then the fun really starts! The metal ball is launched through a series of bumpers, flippers, tracks, and holes to earn points. Improvements to pinball machines over the years made it even more fun to play.

Lights and sounds made games more exciting.

Digital displays and **circuit boards** became standard in pinball machines in the 1970s. Players enjoyed more advanced graphics, lights, and sounds. But by then, Atari had introduced the very popular video game *Pong*. Played on a gaming **console**, it was a simple, tennis-like game that could be played at home.

Ask Questions!

Did your parents or grandparents play pinball when they were younger? What about video games? Ask them what their favorites were.

People would line up to play arcade games.

Digital Gaming

By the early 1980s, video games had replaced most pinball machines at local **arcades**. Animated games like *Asteroids*, *Space Invaders*, and *Pac-Man* earned more money and cost less to maintain.

This was the **golden age** of video games. Companies began developing consoles that could play multiple games from different **cartridges**.

The Nintendo Game Boy launched in 1989.

The early 1990s brought gaming to the home player. More **realistic** graphic images on the screen made gaming more popular than ever. **Portable** handheld gaming devices were introduced.

But the content of video games was soon questioned. People thought that some games were too violent. As a result, the Entertainment Software Rating Board was created in 1994. This organization assigned age and content ratings for video games.

The Legend of Zelda is a popular role-playing game
that is still around today.

The late 1990s saw the explosion of role-playing games (RPGs). An RPG is a game where the player takes on the identity of a specific character. The same video game could be played for multiple hours.

These new video gaming worlds were played with compact discs that offered more storage **capacity**. More storage meant more detailed graphics and more interesting storylines.

Make a Guess!

The next change in how people played video games happened on a small screen. What new device started to include games in the late 1990s?

Today, we have smartphones. What games can you play?

Gaming Online

New cell phones in the late 1990s included "time-killer games." These games were short and simple. They were meant to keep the player busy when they were bored.

Think!

Early cell phone games were very simple. But people wanted to play video games wherever they were. What do you think was the next improvement in video gaming?

The internet offers new game-playing opportunities.

The development of the internet changed gaming forever. Cheap, high-speed connections allow players to connect with others around the world. **Massively multiplayer online (MMO) games** became very popular. MMO games allow players to **interact** with each other in very **complex** gaming worlds.

Video game streaming is the future.

Like music, you will soon **stream** all your video games. Players won't have to spend money on new gaming systems. All you will need is a computer monitor and a **subscription** to a gaming service.

Look!

Video game systems have changed so much over time. Ask an adult to help you search the internet for the timeline of a game system. How does the game system change?

GLOSSARY

arcades (ahr-KAYDZ) places with many games that can be played by putting coins in them

capacity (kuh-PAS-ih-tee) the ability to hold or contain something

cartridges (KAHR-trij-iz) cases that you put into a video game player to play specific games

circuit boards (SUR-kit BORDZ) boards that have many electrical circuits and are used in a piece of electronic equipment

complex (kuhm-PLEKS) very detailed with many parts

console (KAHN-sole) a box that contains the controls for a machine

digital (DIJ-ih-tuhl) using computer technology

golden age (GOHLD-uhn AYJ) a successful period of time

interact (in-tur-AKT) to talk or do things with other people

inventor (in-VEN-tur) someone who creates or produces something useful for the first time

massively multiplayer online games (MAS-iv-lee MUHL-tee-play-ur AWN-line GAYMZ) online games with large numbers of players, on the same server

patented (PAT-uhnt-id) received a legal document that gives the inventor of an item the sole rights to make or sell it for a certain period of time

portable (POR-tuh-buhl) easy to carry or move around

realistic (ree-uh-LIS-tik) very similar to the real thing

stream (STREEM) to get music or video games from the internet without having to download files

subscription (suhb-SKRIP-shuhn) making regular payments for a service

FIND OUT MORE

BOOKS

Go Gaming! The Ultimate Guide to the World's Greatest Mobile Games. New York, NY: Scholastic, Inc., 2016.

Rossignoli, Marco. *The Complete Pinball Book: Collecting the Game and Its History*. North Atglen, PA: Schiffer Publishing, Ltd., 2011.

WEBSITES

PBS Kids—Fetch! Activities: Pinball Wizard
http://www.pbs.org/parents/fetch/activities/act/act-pinball.html
Make your own pinball machine.

Wonderopolis—Who Invented the First Video Game?
https://wonderopolis.org/wonder/who-invented-the-first-video-game
Learn more about the creation of the first video game.

INDEX

ABOUT THE AUTHOR

Jennifer Colby is a school librarian in Ann Arbor, Michigan. She loves reading, traveling, and going to museums to learn about new things.